Octopuses

Octopuses

A Carolrhoda Nature Watch Book

by Ron Hirschi

Carolrhoda Books,   eapolis

To my cousin, Tom, with thanks

Text copyright © 2000 by Ron Hirschi

Carolrhoda Books, Inc.
A division of Lerner Publishing Group
241 First Avenue North
Minneapolis, MN 55401 U.S.A.

Website address: www.lernerbooks.com

Library of Congress Cataloging-in-Publication Data

Hirschi, Ron.
     Octopuses / by Ron Hirschi.
        p.   cm.
     "A Carolrhoda nature watch book."
     Includes index.
     Summary: Describes the physical characteristics, diet,
natural habitat, and life cycle of octopuses.
     ISBN 1-57505-386-1 (lib. bdg. : alk. paper)
     1. Octopodidae—Juvenile literature. [1. Octopus.] I.
Title.
QL430.3.02H57 2000
594'.56—dc21
                                                    99-55098

Manufactured in the United States of America
2 3 4 5 6 7 – JR – 06 05 04 03 02 01

CONTENTS

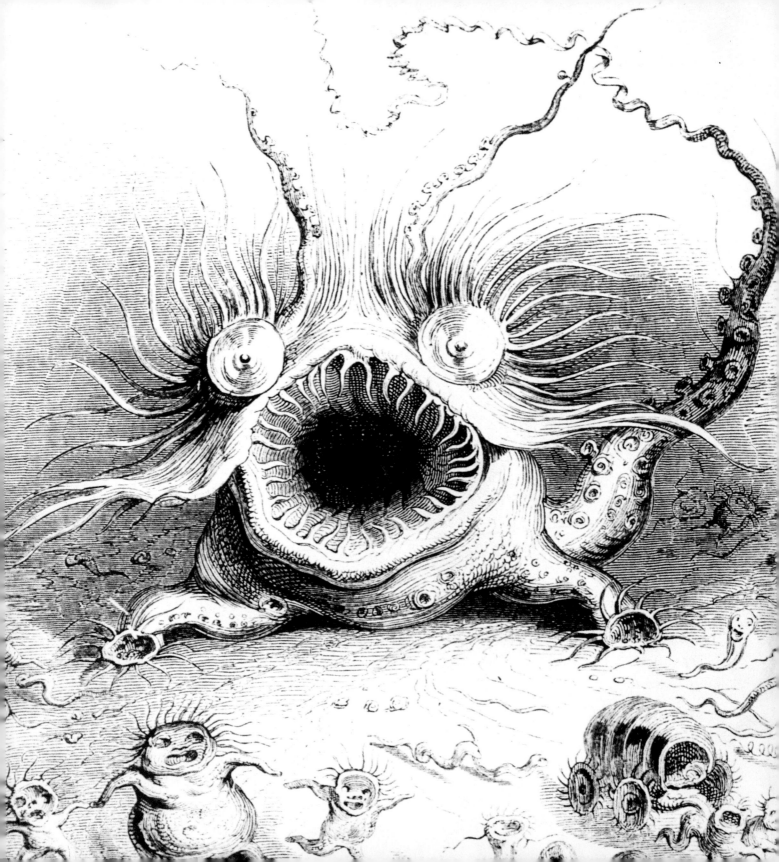

Before the invention of diving equipment, which allowed divers to look at and study sea creatures, artists used their imagination to create underwater monsters.

THEY CALLED IT DEVILFISH

Long ago, people did not have the equipment needed to dive into the depths of the ocean to study sea creatures. In those days, artists illustrated stories about mysterious deep-sea creatures from their imagination, not from photos or face-to-face experience. The stories and drawings sometimes portrayed creatures larger and scarier than they really were.

Once in a while, a dead octopus would wash ashore. Tossed onto the beach by waves, the long arms attached to a fleshy blob would look quite unlike its living, swimming self. It was hard to imagine what this tangle of long arms and soft body would have looked like while alive and underwater.

"There's a devil of a fish!" someone must have said. The name spread far and wide, and stories about the size of this sea creature grew and grew. Legends arose about giant devilfish that crawled onto the beach to curl their long arms around their victims—including people. Anything and anyone unlucky enough to get in the path of this sea monster was sure to disappear.

Early in this century, scientists invented the equipment needed to dive to the depths of the ocean and observe, as well as photograph, octopuses in their natural environment. They learned that octopuses are **invertebrates,** animals that lack backbones. Biologists soon discovered many **species,** or kinds, of octopuses. A few octopus species make their homes deep in the ocean, but most live in fairly shallow water, close to shore.

Some octopuses grow big enough to be called "sea monsters," as legends claimed, while others are smaller than your hand. The smallest octopus is the male dwarf octopus, which grows to only a little more than 1 inch (2.5 cm) from arm tip to arm tip. The Pacific giant is the largest species. Biologists disagree on its ultimate size, but many believe Pacific giant octopuses grow to 20 feet (6 m) or more from arm tip to arm tip and weigh more than 100 pounds (45 kg). This large inhabitant of the sea can live to be 4 or 5 years old. Most octopus species live only 1 year.

Big or small, the octopus is a creature that fascinates people. Like whales and porpoises, octopuses are highly adapted to life in the sea. They are intelligent and curious—and may even inspect humans who swim nearby. If frightened, octopuses will swim away in a blur, squirting a stream of liquid ink to hide their whereabouts. To find them once again, you must look very closely—octopuses can change their body color and texture to blend into their surroundings.

Some octopuses (above) *only grow to about an inch (2.5 cm), while others, like this Pacific giant octopus (below), can grow up to 20 feet (6 m).*

Suckers that line each arm of the octopus help it hold on to objects.

WHAT IS AN OCTOPUS?

Imagine waking to find eight arms sprouting from your body. What would you do with the extras? Could you play better baseball? Could you play piano, strum a guitar, and plink on a banjo while beating a drum?

Each day, healthy octopuses wake up with eight arms. If an arm is torn off by a **predator**—an animal that hunts and eats other animals—the octopus simply regenerates, or grows, a new arm. None of the arms have hands or fingers. So how do octopuses grasp objects? Octopus arms are as flexible as a cat's tail. These flexible arms wrap around objects, while the suction disks, or suckers, that line each arm help the octopus hang on.

10

A hard shell protects the soft body of an abalone (above) *and a snail* (right).

Octopuses belong to a large group of animals called **mollusks,** which include abalone, clams, snails, and even the slippery, slimy garden slug. Mollusks are soft-bodied creatures without backbones. Most mollusks have a hard shell that acts as a protective covering. Octopuses' shells are much smaller, however, and are usually located inside their soft body. There are more mollusk species (about 100,000 different kinds) than any other animal group, with the exception of the incredibly abundant insects.

Along with squid and cuttlefish, octopuses belong to a smaller group of mollusks called **cephalopods.** A cephalopod is a creature with a soft body and many arms. The word *Cephalopoda* comes from the Greek words meaning "head" and "foot." The octopus's "feet" are its eight arms, which are attached to its "head."

A soft layer of skin called a **mantle** covers most of the octopus's body. The mantle surrounds the octopus's organs and forms a hollow area, called the **mantle cavity,** around its gills. To breathe, the octopus uses a pair of tube-like openings called **funnel tubes,** which are found at the base of the octopus's head, to pull seawater inside the mantle cavity. Here, oxygen is taken from the water as it flows against the gills. As the octopus exhales, the funnel tubes push water out.

The squid (above) *and cuttlefish* (right) *are relatives of the octopus.*

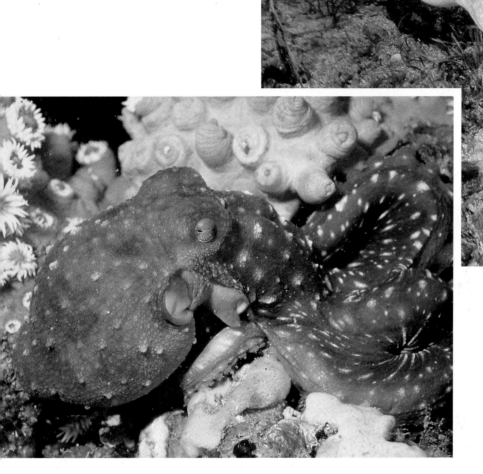

(Left) *An octopus uses its funnel tubes to pull seawater into its mantle cavity, where oxygen is taken from the water.*
(Above) *With arms trailing behind, an octopus pushes water through its funnel tubes to jet through the water.*

An octopus can also use its funnel tubes for quick bursts of speed as it travels about in its underwater home. To do this, the octopus tightens the strong muscles of its mantle, trapping water inside the hollow cavity. Then, with a sudden blast, the octopus pushes the water out through its funnel tubes. This propels the octopus through the water, long arms trailing in a streamlined motion.

The octopus can use this same jet propulsion in shorter, gentler bursts. It swims slowly and elegantly in this way. Then it might drop to the seafloor, where it uses its arms to pull and push its way along.

13

Octopuses' large eyes (inset) *are located on either side of their head* (above).

Unlike most invertebrates, the octopus has a large brain and large eyes. The brain helps the octopus decide if what it sees is friend, foe, or food. Octopus eyes, like human eyes, see brightness, shape, and the size of objects.

Octopus eyes have especially high **acuity** levels, meaning their eyes can focus sharply. Acuity is what helps an eagle see tiny ground squirrels while circling high above the land. Like the eagle and other predators, the octopus uses its keen eyesight to spot its **prey,** or the animals it eats. Some sea creatures may find it hard to spot abalone among the seaweed and snails in the sand, but they are fair game for the hungry octopus.

Although this octopus lives in a brightly colored coral reef, it can see only in black and white.

Several kinds of octopuses hunt after sundown, and others live in deep water where light is very dim. Night vision helps these species see in the dark. As sunlight dims, their pupils dilate, or get larger. The wider pupils help the eyes gather what little light is available.

Though able to see in very dim light, the octopus eye lacks color receptors, the nerve cells needed for color vision. This means that the octopus might live in a spectacular coral reef with splashes of red, blue, and shimmering purple-green, but it cannot see any of those colors. No matter how much sunlight is available, an octopus sees only in black and white.

A reef-dwelling octopus hides from its enemies and watches for prey in the safety of a coral-reef den.

Deep-sea octopuses, like this flapjack devilfish, generally have softer bodies than reef dwellers.

WHERE DO OCTOPUSES LIVE?

The octopus has evolved, or slowly changed, over many thousands of years. It lives in every ocean, but none exist in freshwater. Most of the 200 species hug the seafloor or dwell in reefs and rocks in fairly shallow water along the coast. An octopus's typical **habitat,** or place where it naturally lives, has rocks or coral clusters for hiding and hunting. But some live on sandy seafloors, in great depths.

Little is known about octopuses that dwell in the deepest parts of the sea. Biologists do know that deep-sea octopuses are generally softer bodied than reef dwellers. These octopuses, like the Dumbo octopus, usually have a webbing between their arms that stretches as the arms move. The webbing helps the octopuses swim through the water.

In shallower water, many octopuses make their homes in coral reefs. Biologists have learned a great deal about them. Octopuses make their homes, called **dens**, in small spaces, like a crack in a rock or a gap in a coral reef. But they also use discarded pots, barrels, or cans. Any tight space will do for a hideaway, but the area surrounding an octopus's home must be rich in food.

Like a garbage can outside a doorway, broken shells often litter a den opening. These shells are the remains of octopus dinners, tossed out after the tender parts have been eaten. Divers search for entrances to dens by looking for these piles of discarded shells.

Top: *Empty shells litter the opening of an octopus's den.*
Left: *A parrot fish uses its sharp teeth to eat the algae that grows on coral reefs, helping to shape the octopuses' home.*

An octopus hunts for clams, abalone, crabs, and fish along coral and sand.

Octopuses are dependent on other animals to help shape their reef homes. One of the most important is the parrot fish. Its strong teeth help the parrot fish to crunch and munch on **algae,** or underwater plants, that grow on the harder, nonliving parts of a coral reef. As the parrot fish crunches algae, it also eats bits of coral. When digested and eliminated, the coral bits create sandy hiding places in inner parts of the reef. Clams, abalone, crabs, and fish—sea creatures that octopuses eat—make their homes there. Octopuses often hunt in these sandy inner parts.

Wind and water also shape octopus habitat. Some octopuses live in deeper waters on the outside edges of a reef. Here, waves pound the coral and reshape the rich, colorful habitat. This creates new hiding places for prey animals.

Two kinds of octopuses live in the reefs found in Hawaii. One species is commonly called the day octopus and the other is called the night octopus. Both are known as the *he'e* in Hawaiian, a name that means "to slide along or flee."

The day he'e reaches about 2 feet (0.6 m) in width. This small octopus is brown or gray and is well known in the islands for its sharp beak, which can inflict a painful bite if the octopus is picked up. The night he'e is slightly smaller and wears a striking pattern of white spots on its reddish body and arms.

The day he'e (top) *and the night he'e* (bottom)

Another rich and colorful octopus habitat is found along the coast of the Pacific Northwest. Here, kelp plants (the largest marine algae) grow into huge forests. Giant kelp plants attach to rocks on the seafloor. The plants extend up from their anchoring place, growing as much as 4 inches (10 cm) each day. No plant community grows so quickly or provides as much food and shelter for so many sea creatures. Among the octopuses living here is the Pacific giant octopus. It makes its home near Seattle, Washington.

Left: *Kelp plants anchor themselves to rocks and grow quickly.*
Above: *Forests of kelp plants provide shelter for octopuses and other sea creatures.*

21

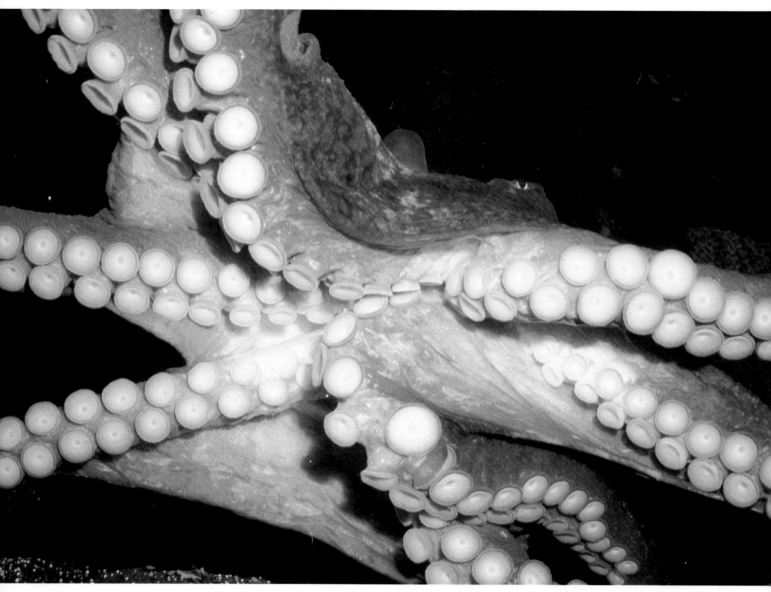

An octopus can taste and feel with its suckers, helping it to find food and escape enemies.

FINDING FOOD

Imagine going to the refrigerator at night after a storm has shut off the power to your home. If you had to feel around in the dark for a snack, the smooth skin of an apple might feel the same as the outside of an onion. But if you could taste with your fingertips, you could avoid biting into the wrong one.

Octopuses must search for food in dark places on many occasions. Some species always hunt at night, some inhabit murky waters, and others frequent deep seas where sunlight does not penetrate. Luckily, the octopus can actually taste with its suckers. Nerves that line each of the suckers send "flavor" messages to the brain. The taste receptors on each sucker help the octopus sample its surroundings for tasty prey. Each sucker also has many nerves that give the octopus a highly sensitive sense of touch.

The octopus can tell the shape and texture of clams, rocks, shrimp, and other animals or objects. This ability helps the octopus find food and avoid enemies, even in the darkest sea cave.

Dumbo octopuses, like many deep-sea octopuses, are cirrate octopuses. A cirrate octopus has rows of bristlelike hairs called **cirri,** as well as suckers, on its arms that help it find food. Sensitive to touch, cirri assist in searching for prey on the dark seafloor. The bristles also help the octopus catch food. Like miniature brooms, the cirri sweep small animals into the octopus's mouth.

Another deep-sea octopus is the flapjack devilfish. The flapjack stretches its arms wide, pounces on its prey, and traps small sea creatures beneath its outstretched flaps. Then its cirri sweep the catch into the devilfish's mouth.

Bristlelike hairs, called cirri, line the flapjack devilfish's arms.

Above: *Clams have a tough outer shell that helps protect them from most predators.*
Top right: *Can you spot the octopus hiding in the rocks?*

Camouflage, or blending in with its surroundings, also aids the octopus in capturing its prey. Many animals find their way into the cracks and crevices of a coral reef, and unsuspecting crabs or shrimp often mistake an octopus arm for seaweed or coral until it's too late.

Snails and clams may be easy to catch, but their thick, hard shells are not easy to crack. The octopus mouth looks a lot like a parrot's beak. Inside is a rough tongue called a **radula.** Octopuses use the raspy radula to drill through the hard shells of even the largest snails, such as the conch.

Biologists have observed some octopuses eating conch snails at a very slow pace. The octopus seizes the snail and turns it so that the octopus can drill a hole into the spiral end. It drills through the shell at a speed of about 0.04 inches (1 mm) per hour. The octopus then injects a poison into the soft parts of the snail. The injected poison weakens the snail, and its body falls away from the shell. Then the conch dinner is ready to be swallowed. Since a conch shell can be several millimeters thick, a single meal might take more than 3 hours to prepare.

Other snails, oysters, clams, and hard-shelled crabs are eaten in a similar fashion, using the octopus's poison to prepare the food. But the octopus's strong beak can tear softer prey into bite-sized chunks. Fish, squid, starfish, sea cucumbers, shrimp, fish eggs, and other octopuses are all part of the octopus diet.

A hard-shelled crab

The blue-ringed octopus is small, but deadly.

One of the most beautiful octopuses, the blue-ringed octopus, carries a poison lethal to humans as well as sea creatures. The blue-ringed octopus grows to only 4 inches (10 cm) in width, but its tiny size is respected by divers who explore its Australian reef habitat. One blue-ringed octopus packs enough poison to kill ten adult humans. Death comes to the victim as quickly as 2 hours after a bite. By stunning prey with its poison, this small, electric-blue octopus is able to capture prey larger than itself.

ESCAPING ENEMIES

Hungry sharks, moray eels, and barracudas hunt octopuses. Since its soft body parts are not protected by a hard shell or strong bones, the octopus is especially vulnerable. But the octopus is a clever escape artist.

Octopuses avoid many predators simply by hiding in their dens or small crevices in a reef or rock. For example, the night he'e escapes many enemies by tucking its body into a tight space during the day. At night, it uses the cover of dark seas to go about its hunting. But he'e octopuses need to be on the lookout for barracudas, ulua, sharks, and moray eels—these predators make meals of day and night octopuses.

An octopus (left) *hides in its narrow den from predators, such as the barracuda* (below).

The moray eel tries to catch octopuses by sneaking into the crevices where octopuses hide. Morays all have the same basic body shape—long, slender, and snakelike—just right for fitting into an octopus den. To help avoid capture, an octopus may change color to match its surroundings. It can also change its skin texture.

Slippery like chocolate sauce atop ice cream, octopus skin is loose fitting. Tiny fibers attach it to the stronger muscles underneath. This delicate fiber layer is a kind of remote control center filled with organs called **chromatophores.** The chromatophores are filled with tiny sacks of color **pigments.** Certain brain impulses can signal a change in skin color, while others signal a change in skin texture. This allows an octopus to turn from brown to red while its skin turns smooth or rough and bumpy.

The moray eel, like the octopus, can fit into tight crevices.

Above: *An octopus blends into its surroundings.*
Left: *An octopus squirts a cloud of ink to muddy the waters and escape from a predator.*

Should an octopus be spotted by a tiger shark or other predator that might chase it, the octopus can squirt a cloud of ink as an unusual defense. This ink jet is puffed out through its funnel tubes. Sometimes the ink forms a cloud, but amazingly, some octopuses can squirt ink to form a shape similar to their own. This ink decoy can fool some hungry predators long enough for the octopus to escape.

The sea otter will search everywhere—from discarded pots to aluminum cans—on the sea floor for octopuses to eat.

Not all octopus predators hunt by sight. Some, such as sea otters, are especially clever. Otters dive down to find dinners of octopuses, urchins, abalone, and other animals found in kelp forests. Biologists have even seen sea otters check for octopuses in aluminum cans that litter the ocean floor. If an otter finds an octopus hiding inside, it swims with the can to the surface. The otter tears apart the aluminum with its teeth and nimble paws and dines on its canned meal.

Mammals such as river otters, elephant seals, sea lions, harbor seals, and the rare Hawaiian monk seal also feed on octopuses. In deeper waters, lancetfish, with their fanglike teeth, feed on octopuses and squid.

Lingcod and halibut, large bottom-dwelling fish, also feed on octopuses and share some of their many-legged prey's behaviors. Both fish hide their bulky bodies by blending in with the surrounding sand. Halibut are so fond of eating octopuses that people who fish use octopus bait or lures to catch halibut.

Sea otters search kelp forests, like this one, for octopuses and other sea creatures.

Two male octopuses reach with their hectocotylus arms to mate with a female.

LIFE CYCLE

The mating ritual can be quite spectacular for many octopuses. Usually, octopuses live by themselves. During the mating season, rival males fight off others that approach a female. When a male approaches a female, his courtship includes a flash of color changes. In some species, a male will also reach out an arm and gently stroke the female.

If the female accepts, the male draws nearer. A male may take as long as half an hour to transfer sperm using his **hectocotylus** arm. Separate from the other arms, it is coiled inside a bulblike sac. Once developed, the sac bursts and the arm is released. Longer and more slender than the other arms, the hectocotylus extends like a whip. During mating, the male uses his hectocotylus to take a sperm packet from his body. He inserts the packet into the female's mantle cavity. Here, egg and sperm unite and the fertilized eggs soon begin to develop. The male and female then separate and follow very different paths. The male swims away to find additional mates. But the female swims in search of a safe place to deposit her developing eggs.

The soft shell worn by the female paper nautilus is used as an egg case and a protective covering.

Courtship and mating behavior vary greatly among octopus species. Most unusual is the paper nautilus. A female paper nautilus grows to about 1 foot (0.3 m) in length, while males grow to no more than 1 inch (2.5 cm). Females wear a kind of shell, but it is softer than a clam or snail shell. Young females begin to build the covering when as young as 12 days old. When they mature, the shell becomes a case for their eggs.

A male paper nautilus looks much more like other octopuses. But unlike most male octopuses, when the male paper nautilus uses his hectocotylus arm to insert his sperm packet into the female, the arm breaks away from his body. Both the sperm packet and the arm remain inside the female's mantle cavity.

This blue-ringed octopus has attached her eggs to her body to protect them from predators.

After mating, most female octopuses lay eggs. One exception is *Ocythoe tuberculata,* a species that lives in the Pacific and Atlantic Oceans. *O. tuberculata* females may reach lengths of about 1 foot (0.3 m). Their eggs develop inside the female's body and she gives birth to live, fully formed baby octopuses.

In the deep sea, cirrate octopuses, such as the Dumbo octopus, tuck their eggs beneath the wide webbing in their arms. Since they live in sandy, open areas with no rocky reefs for protection, Dumbo mothers must hide their eggs from predators until the eggs hatch.

Many female octopus species attach their eggs to the ceiling of a den.

Octopus mothers spend all their time washing and guarding their eggs.

Other egg-laying species may search for caves or seashells to shelter their eggs. To protect the eggs from being swept away by water currents, a mother octopus uses a kind of glue on each tiny egg. Some octopuses individually glue their eggs to rock, shell, or coral. Others attach the eggs to each other in clusters that look like bunches of grapes.

Octopus eggs are soft. Depending on the species, the female may produce as many as 100,000 eggs. The eggs are guarded by the mother. She keeps the eggs clean by squirting water over them with her funnel tubes. The water also helps oxygen reach the developing young inside the thin eggs.

In many species, mother octopuses don't eat for the entire time the eggs are developing, a process that might last as long as 3 to 5 months. Since many octopuses live only 1 year, motherhood lasts as much as a quarter of a female's entire life. In these short-lived species, the mother's life ends before or at the time the babies hatch. Then the octopus babies are swept away into the surrounding sea to live on their own.

When hatched, the baby is fully formed, a miniature version of its parents with all eight legs, a bulblike head, and a tiny but sharp mouth. Its life at this stage is poorly understood, but biologists have found baby octopuses in the open ocean, well above the seafloor. Soon, however, the small octopuses settle to the seafloor, where they inhabit rocky crevices, reefs, or sandy bottoms similar to adult habitats.

Octopuses begin to break out of their transparent eggs.

A lot needs to be learned before biologists can say much more about the early life of most octopuses. Biologists have studied one species, the Pacific giant octopus, fairly closely. At birth, giant octopus babies are only about as big as a pencil's eraser. Mothers attend the eggs in a sea cave until they hatch. On hatching, the baby giants swim and drift as **plankton,** or small sea life that drifts in ocean currents, for about 2 months.

A newly hatched Pacific giant octopus is about the size of a pencil's eraser.

A young night octopus swims and drifts in ocean currents. As it grows older, it will settle to the seafloor and grow quickly.

During the planktonic life stage, many Pacific giant octopuses become prey of animals ranging from fish to whales. But by the time they settle to the seafloor, giant octopuses grow quickly and avoid predators by blending into their surroundings, squirting ink, and using their jet power. At 1 year, they weigh about 1 pound (454 g) and live in fairly shallow water, often in areas exposed at low tide. At this time, you might uncover a baby giant beneath an algae-covered rock in a tide pool.

By a year and a half, the little giants weigh 5 or 6 pounds (2.3–2.7 kg). They gradually move into deeper waters, but even the largest will occasionally appear in very shallow water. When males are 1 year old and females are 2 or 3 years old, Pacific giant octopuses are ready to mate and produce their own young. The cycle of life continues.

A street vendor sells octopuses at a market in Yokosuka, Japan.

PEOPLE AND OCTOPUSES

Octopuses have fascinated curious people for many centuries. Long before people were able to dive deep into the oceans to learn about their wide range of habitats and habits, many people relied on octopuses for food. Octopuses are still an important seafood to many people. Italian, Greek, and Spanish people have had especially long histories of octopus fishing. Cookbooks from these countries often include recipes for preparing octopus. Octopuses are eaten raw, steamed, or smoked. Thinly sliced octopus is a common ingredient in Japanese sushi. Its texture and taste is similar to clams.

A fisher displays a large octopus he caught while out at sea on the Oregon coast.

People all over the world capture octopuses in many ways. In the Hawaiian and other Pacific Islands, people catch octopuses with spears, traps, and cowrie lures. A cowrie has a soft body and a hard outer shell. Using empty cowrie shells as bait, people can catch octopuses. Following the example of sea otters, Europeans catch octopuses in clay or ceramic pots. A line with many pots is dropped into the water, then retrieved later.

Northern Africans have also caught octopuses for many years, but they often catch their many-legged seafood in nets. Trawls—nets pulled behind a boat—are dragged on the seafloor, scooping up octopuses, often in great numbers.

Thousands of people enjoy watching octopuses in their natural habitat. Divers and snorkelers spend many hours watching and photographing octopuses. Diving guidebooks often point out locations where you might find these popular reef animals.

Aquariums keep octopuses for people's enjoyment and for study. But one of the first things octopus keepers learn is that octopuses may try to escape. They have a habit of crawling out of their tanks, so octopus aquariums must design their enclosures with care. Octopuses have even been known to crawl from one tank to another during the night.

Biologists watch octopuses in aquariums to learn about their intelligence and habits.

The age of an octopus can be determined by counting the growth rings on its statoliths, located inside its body.

Through aquarium and natural habitat study, biologists have learned that they can calculate the age of an octopus by counting its growth rings, similar to counting a tree's rings. Each year, a tree produces a ring just inside its bark. An octopus produces rings each day. The rings are found on its **statoliths,** small balls of calcium located inside its body that the octopus uses for balance. Biologists slice thin wafers of statoliths to count the rings. Gathering samples from octopuses in different locations helps to paint a picture of the movements of the animals as they grow and age.

Researchers at the Seattle Aquarium conducted experiments proving that their Pacific giant octopuses play. Much like ping-pong players, the octopuses will "bounce" an object back and forth using jets of water from their funnel tubes. Other biologists have watched octopuses unscrew jar lids. The intelligence of these animals suggests they are capable of much more.

Unfortunately, octopus research is lagging behind studies of many other sea animals. Studies of fish such as sharks, swordfish, salmon, and many other commercially valuable species usually get the most research money. From their research, biologists have found that many of these fish are at risk of extinction. This is due in part to modern, highly efficient netting on the open seas. Often, a variety of fish and other sea life are unintentionally caught in nets meant to catch only specific species. This accidental harvest is known as "by-catch" and can be a serious threat to entire species. Little is known about unintentional catches of octopuses. Recent studies have shown that some nets are accidentally killing many octopus relatives, causing concern that by-catch may be threatening populations of many sea creatures.

People still have much to learn about octopuses, and close study in aquariums and natural habitat is ongoing. What are the habitat needs of newly hatched octopuses? What are the populations of the various octopus species? How are their numbers being affected by commercial fishing and human destruction of coral reefs? Biologists are working hard to unlock these and other answers. But they have a long way to go. Just imagine—you might be the one to discover more of the octopus's abilities and protect its future.

GLOSSARY

acuity: a measure of the eye's ability to focus

algae: a group of underwater plants of many sizes, lacking the usual roots, branches, and leaves of trees and flowers

camouflage: to blend in with surroundings

cephalopods: creatures with soft bodies and many arms

chromatophores: tiny, color-filled sacs in fish, octopuses, and other animals. The mixing of the color pigments within the chromatophores helps these animals change colors and patterns.

cirri: small, bristlelike growths such as those on the arms of a cirrate octopus. Cirri are controlled by muscles and aid in finding and catching food.

dens: cavelike dwellings in reefs or other seafloor structures, where octopuses hide, feed, or lay eggs

funnel tubes: tubelike openings found at the base of an octopus's head

habitat: the kind of environment in which a species normally lives

hectocotylus: a special arm some male cephalopods use in mating

invertebrates: animals that lack backbones

mantle: a layer of skin covering the main part of an octopus's body

mantle cavity: a water-filled space within an octopus's body

mollusks: soft-bodied creatures without backbones, including snails, clams, and octopuses

pigments: the colorings found in the skin of some cephalopods

plankton: plants or animals living as free-floating creatures. Some are too small to be seen without the use of a microscope.

predator: an animal that hunts and eats other animals

prey: an animal that is killed and eaten by other animals

radula: a raspy tongue found in the mouth of octopuses and many other mollusks

species: a kind of animal or plant. Members of the same species can mate and produce young that are like their parents.

statoliths: small balls of calcium located inside an octopus's body, used for balance

INDEX

ABOUT THE AUTHOR

Ron Hirschi has been fascinated with life in the water from his earliest explorations in Puget Sound, home of the largest known octopus. He studied ecology at the University of Washington and became interested in writing when he began reading children's books to his daughter, Nichol. He has since written more than three dozen books, including many award-winning titles. Ron has worked as a fisheries biologist and is especially interested in protecting and restoring habitats important to freshwater and marine life. Much of his free time is spent fishing or swimming in search of fish and other sealife, including the octopus. Ron and his wife, Brenda, live with their two dogs and one cat on Marrowstone Island, not far from where he saw his first octopus as a child.